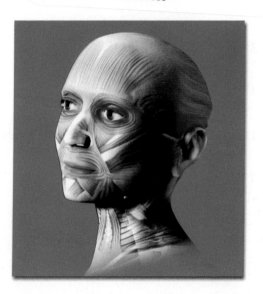

The Skeleton and Muscles

Ben Williams

Table of Contents

The Skeleton and Muscles

Imagine that you had no skeleton or muscles. How would you stand? How would you move? How would you throw a ball, touch your toes, or even blink your eyes?

The answer is that you could not do any
of those things. You need a skeleton and
muscles to do all the things you want to do.

Your skeleton and muscles work together. They help you keep your shape, and they allow you to move.

All About the Skeleton

If you look at yourself in the mirror, you can get a good idea of what your skeleton is like under your skin.

Bones are inside every part of your body. Bones connect together to make your skeleton, and your skeleton gives you your size and shape.

Joints

If bones are connected, how can they move? Bones are connected with joints that let them move in different directions.

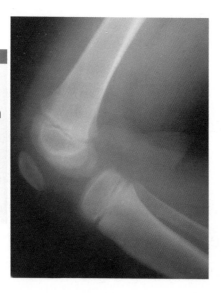

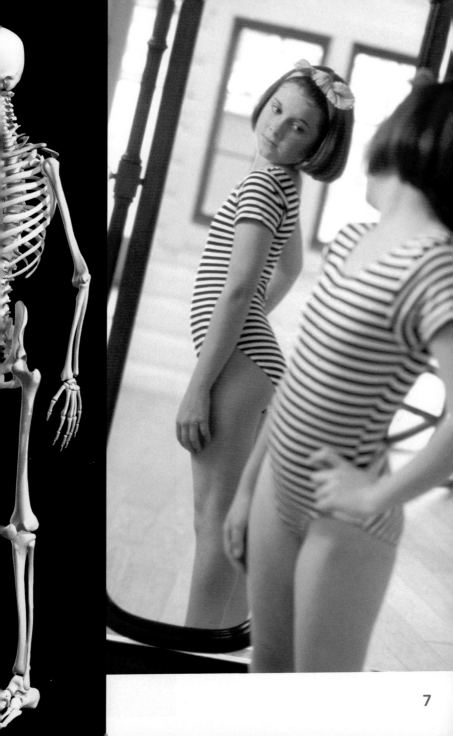

Each bone in your body has its own important job to do.

Skull Bones

The skull looks like one bone, but it is really made of 28 bones. The skull bones connect like the pieces of a puzzle.

Some bones protect you. Your **skull** is one of those bones. It protects your brain.

Some bones give you shape. Your **ribs** make the shape of your chest. They protect your heart, lungs, stomach, and liver, too.

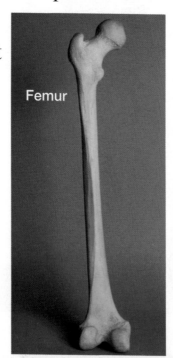

Femur

Some bones give you strength to stand. Your **femur** is the thigh bone. It helps to hold you up.

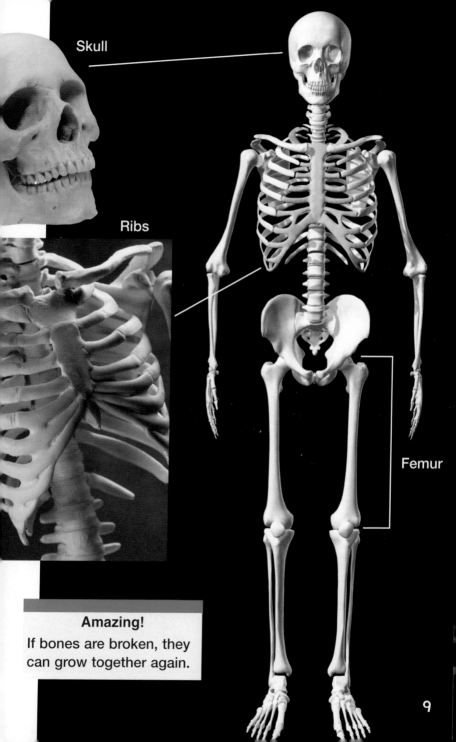

Skull

Ribs

Femur

Amazing!
If bones are broken, they
can grow together again.

9

Bones do something else that is very important. They help to make your blood.

Inside each bone is **marrow**. It is soft like jelly. Bone marrow makes new blood for your body.

Bone material

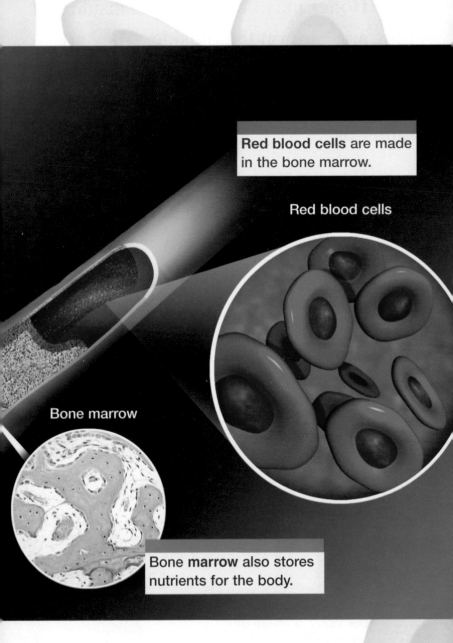

Red blood cells are made in the bone marrow.

Red blood cells

Bone marrow

Bone **marrow** also stores nutrients for the body.

Bones may be soft on the inside, but they are hard on the outside. They are made from some of the same things you can find in rocks! These things are called **minerals**.

Bones are also dry compared to the rest of the body. A large part of your body is made of water, but only a small part of your skeleton is.

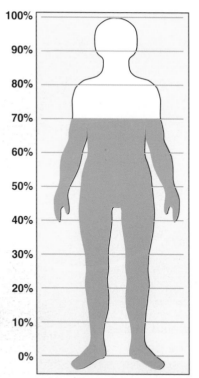

Your body is made of about 70% water

All the bones of your skeleton are connected to each other, except for one. The **thyroid bone** is in your throat, behind your tongue and above your Adam's apple. Muscles hold it there.

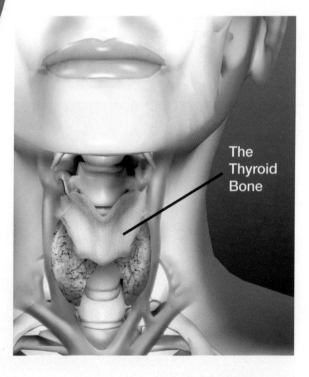

The Thyroid Bone

As you grow older, your body grows bigger. You get more of almost everything as you grow: more teeth, more hair, more height, and more weight.

But, you do not get more bones. In fact, you get less!

Smallest and Biggest

The smallest bone you have is in your ear. It is called the **stapes** (STAY-peez), and it helps you hear. The biggest bone you have is the **femur** (FEE-mur) in your thigh. (On page 8 there is a picture of a femur.)

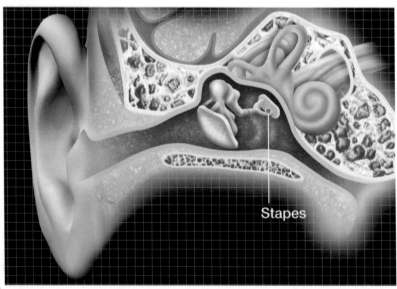

Stapes

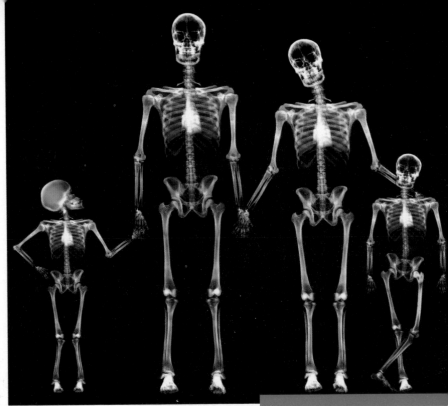

Most bones grow longer and bigger as you grow older, but some bones also grow together into one big bone. So, even though a baby has more than 300 bones, an adult has only 206.

Shrinking!

You are shorter at night than you are in the morning! During the day, gravity causes the bones in your back to close the spaces between them, so you shrink a little. At night, the spaces soak up water, so you get taller again.

All About Muscles

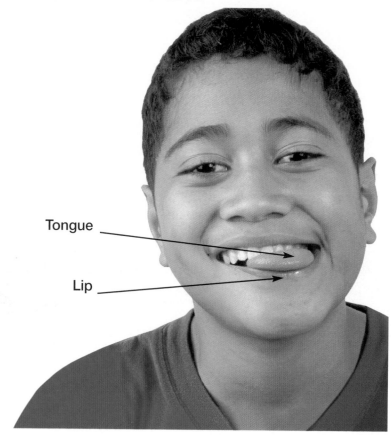

Tongue

Lip

Which of these body parts are made
mostly of muscles?

- •tongue
- •heart
- •lips
- •stomach

Heart

Stomach

Can you guess? The answer is **all of them**! They each have many muscles that help them do their jobs. Without muscles, they would just lie there and do nothing at all.

What exactly are muscles? They are the parts of the body that move bones and make body organs like the heart, lungs, and stomach work. They are also in the walls of blood vessels to make blood move.

There are more than 650 different muscles in your body. That is a lot! Your muscles make up a little less than half of your total weight. So, if you weigh 60 pounds, your muscles weigh about 25 pounds.

Smile!
Did you know that it takes more muscles to frown than to smile?

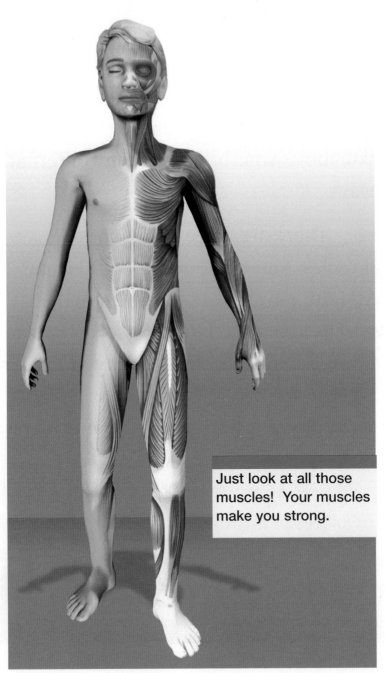

Just look at all those muscles! Your muscles make you strong.

Muscles are made of hundreds or thousands of thin strands called fibers that can stretch and snap back into shape, a little like a rubber band does. This lets you move your bones in many different ways.

There are three main types of muscles: **smooth**, **cardiac**, and **skeletal**. **Smooth muscles** are mostly in body organs and some blood vessels. They do things for your body without you thinking

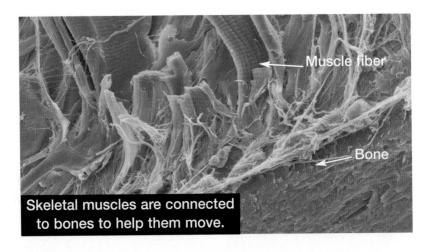

Muscle fiber

Bone

Skeletal muscles are connected to bones to help them move.

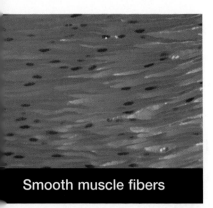

Smooth muscle fibers

Cardiac (KARD-ee-ak) has to do with the heart. **Skeletal** (SKEL-ətəl) has to do with the bones.

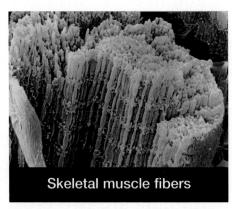

Skeletal muscle fibers

Cardiac muscle fibers

These muscle fibers are dyed different colors to make it easier to see them.

about them, like digest your food and move your blood. **Cardiac muscles** are in the heart. They make your heart pump. **Skeletal muscles** are connected to bones. You use them to move things like your legs, arms, neck, and fingers.

Building Strong Bones and Muscles

How do bones and muscles grow and become stronger? Exercise makes them grow and keeps them fit. The more you use them, the stronger they are and the more energy they have.

You should exercise every day. You can exercise just by playing. Jumping and running are two great ways to keep your bones and muscles strong and healthy.

Hefty!

Muscles allow you to lift heavy things. The most weight any human being has ever lifted is 6,270 pounds. A man named Paul Anderson did that in 1957.

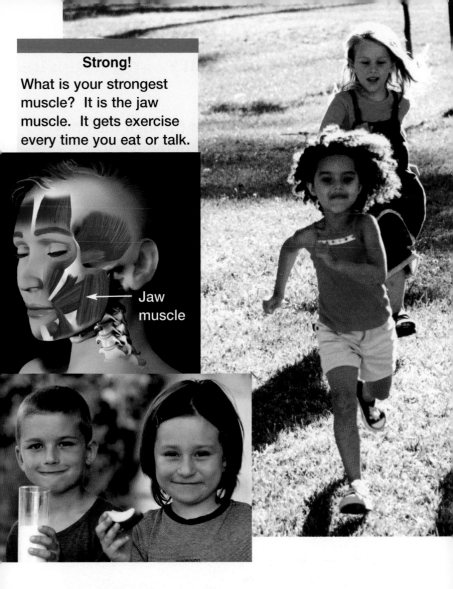

Jaw muscle

Your bones and muscles need good food, too. Good food keeps them strong and helps them to last a long, long time.

23

Glossary

blood vessels   tubes that run through the body to carry blood to and from the heart

exercise   activity to move the body and keep it strong and healthy

gravity   an invisible force that holds people to Earth

joints   places where bones meet, allowing them to move

marrow   the inside of bones that is soft and jelly-like

minerals   combinations of atoms and molecules that form the basic parts of rocks, bones, and other parts of the body

muscles   body parts made of long fibers that stretch and bend, allowing the body and body organs to move

skeleton   the structure of bones that supports, protects, and holds the body in shape